Mayflower
and The

For Two Generations After the Landing

Including

A SHORT HISTORY OF THE
CHURCH OF THE PILGRIM
FOUNDERS OF NEW ENGLAND

Published by
BUREAU OF
MILITARY AND CIVIC ACHIEVEMENT
Washington, D. C.

OLD AND NEW STYLE OF RECKONING:

At the time of the landing of the Pilgrims the new year was reckoned as beginning on the 25th day of March. According to the new style of computation dates of records of those times between 1st January and 25th March should have one year added.

Copyright 1922
by
JOHN T. LANDIS

FOREWORD

The preparation of this booklet is the first instance, so far as known, wherein the data it contains have all been brought together within the covers of a single volume.

While the material appears scattered through famliy histories, published records and genealogical periodicals, it must be observed that its examination under that circumstance has been attended with the difficulty and inconvenience of consulting the different works and various volume-numbers of the periodicals. In view therefore of all the data having been brought together herein in a single booklet, the advantage of ready-reference afforded by the present "Mayflower Descendants and their Marriages for Two Generations" is fully apparent.

No claim is made for literary effort or original authorship, the work in the present instance being that of editing and arrangement of the data with a view to conciseness and ready reference.

For the assistance of those who may desire to extend their investigation beyond the two generations of children, the following reference-index is offered with acknowledgement to those authors who collected their information from original sources.   The Compiler.

List of References

(Such data as are statistical, i. e. consisting merely of names, dates, etc., are necessarily repeated or duplicated in many of the respective publications in so far as the passengers and the first generation or so appear.)

New Eng. Hist. & Gen. Reg.
Savage's Gen. Dict.
Austin's Allied Families.
Spooner Memorial.
Winsor's Hist. Duxbury Mass.
Stile's Hist. of Windsor, Ct.
Wyman's Charlestown Mass. Gens.
N. Y. Gen. & Biog. Record.
Rogers Families of Plymouth.
Bass Family Hist.
Colonial Families of the U. S. of America.

Charlestown Gens. and Estates.
Aldrich's Hist. Windsor Ct.
Hist. New Bedford Mass.
Memorial of Wm. Spooner (—Thomas Spooner).
Huling's Ancestry of Alden Spooner.
New London Co. Hist. Colls.
Life of John Alden.
A Pilgrim Family (— Alden).
Ancestors of Isaac Alden and Irene Smith.
Elihib Alden's Ancestors.
Memorial of the Descendants of Isaac Alden (— Cunner).
Memorial of the Descendants of Hon. John Alden. (— E. Alden. M. D.)
Memorial of the Descendants of Wm. Bradford. (— Fessendon).
Pilgrim Rec. Society Bulletin.
Signers of the Mayflower Compact and their Descdts. (— Whittemore).
Gen. Rec. of the Bradfords, Fullers, Ellises.
Rec. of the Descdts of Wm. Brewster of the Mayflower. (— Jones).
The Doty— Doten Family (— Ethan Allen Doty).
A Mayflower line: Hopkins, Snow, Cook, Eldridge.
Davis' Landmarks of Plymouth.
Thayer Memorial.
Nat. Gen. Quarterly.
Boston Society of the Descdts. of John Howland Quarterly.
The Standishes of America.
Richard Warren and some of his Discds.
Descdts. of Edward Winslow (— Bryant)
Hinman's Ct. Settlers.
Swift's Barnstable Mass. Families.
Chipman's Family Lineage.
Haskell Family Hist.
The Mayflower Descendant Mag.
Mayflower Descdts. in Cape May Co. (— Howe).
Vinton's Giles, and the Gens. of Snow; Chandler; Hatch; Foster; Stoddard; Davis; White; Combs; Sherman; Bonney; Delano; Walker; Payne and Gore; Baxter; Sampson; Weston; Cushman; Spooner; Swift; Soule and Terry.

Ye Compacte
Signed in Ye Cabin of Ye Mayflower
Ye 11 of November
Anno Dominie 1620

In ye name of God, Amen.—We whofe names are underwrtitten, the loyall subjects of our dread and foveraigne Lord, King James, by ye grace of God, of Great Britaine, France, & Yreland king, defender of ye faith. &c., haveing undertaken for ye glorie of God, and advancemente of ye Christian faith, and honour to our king and countrie, a voyage to plant ye first colonie in ye Northerne parts of Virginia, doe by thefe prefents solemnly and mutually in ye prefense of God, and one of another, covenant and combine ourfelves togeather into a civill body politick, for our better ordering & prefervation & furtherance of ye ends aforesaid; and by vertue hearof to enacte, conftitute, and frame fuch just & equall lawes, ordinances, Acts, conftitutions, & offices from time to time, as fhall be thought most meete & convenient for ye generall goode of ye Colonie, unto which we promife all due submiffiion and obedience. Yn witnefs whereof we have hereunder subfcribed our names at Cap-Codd ye 11. of November, in ye year of ye raigne of our soveraigne lord, King James, of England, France, & Yreland ye eighteenth, and Scotland ye fiftie fourth, Ano: Dom. 1620.

John Carver	William Bradford
Edward Winflow	William Brewfter
Ifaac Allerton	Myles Standifh
John Alden	Samuel Fuller
Chriftopher Martin	William Mullins
William White	Richard Warren
John Howland	Stephen Hopkins
Edward Tilley	John Tilley
Francif Cooke	Thomas Rogers
Thomas Tinker	John Rigdale
Edward Fuller	John Turner
Francis Eaton	James Chilton
John Cracfton	John Billington
Mofes Fletcher	John Goodman
Degory Prieft	Thomas Williams
Gilbert Winflow	Edmond Margefon
Peter Brown	Richard Britterige
— George Soule	Richard Clark
Richard Gardiner	John Allerton
Thomas Englifh	Edward Doty
	Edward Leifter

A SHORT HISTORY OF THE CHURCH OF THE PILGRIM FOUNDERS OF NEW ENGLAND

By John Tannehill Landis

Member of

New York Genealogical and Biographical Society.
American Historical Association.
California Genealogical Society
Baronial Order of Runnemede.
National Genealogical Society.
Maryland Historical Society.
Tennessee Historical Society.
Scions of Colonial Cavaliers.
Virginia Historical Society.
Military Order of Pulaski.
Order of the Yellow Rose.
Order of Oglethorpe.
Order of Washington.
Order of LaFayette.

The Reformation in the 16th Century set at liberty in the minds of men a great diversity of free-thought and action in religious affairs. A result was that the widely divergent views thus brought into existence chrystalized into settled opinions of doctrine that gave much difficulty, when, subsequently, it was sought for political reasons to form National Churches.

In the first phase of this great religious revolution England had broken away from the Church of Rome, under Henry VIII. This period, which has been called the negative, was followed by one more spiritual in the reign of Edward VI, becoming reactionary under Queen Mary, and finally resulting in the establishment of the Protestant Church of England under Queen Elizabeth.

Opposition to retaining the old time uniformity of faith and ordinances and the display of ceremonial, by those who held as a principle that there was nothing good in the ancient Church, and condemned any semblance of its practices as a relic of popery, had advanced to the point where severe strictures were placed by the authorities on non-conformity with the tenets of the National Church of England.

The Rev. Joseph Hunter tells us in his "Collections Regarding the Congregation of Protestant Separatists," that England had at that time "many families who adhered in principle and in heart to the ancient, and then abrogated, system which was remembered by them with affectionate reverence touching its ceremonies and rituals." However the non-comformists separated into numerous independent bodies of Separatists, or Congregationalists, as they were called, and continued their efforts to exercise that freedom of conscience and simplicity of worship which they so stoutly advocated despite the "Acts of Royal Supremacy and Uniformity" issued in 1559, designed to enforce a uniformity of religious doctrine and modes of worship.

A subsequent split in the Separatists resulted in the Presbyterian and the Brownist Churches, from whom came the Pilgrim Fathers.

The Rev. Joseph Hunter says, further, "that besides being formed on the Scripture model, and that those who belonged to them escaped from the tyranny of the authorities in the English Church, they had two other advantages — facility in excluding immoral persons from church fellowship, and the liberty of making fresh changes in opinion or practice should fresh light break in upon them."

He tells us also that it was one of these Communities of Puritan Separatists, formed in the county village of Scrooby in North Nottinghamshire, that laid the foundation for New Plymouth, the parent colony of New England.

Resolving to seek in some other country that protection and toleration denied them at home, Holland, a country at no great distance, was settled upon by the Scrooby Congregation as a refuge where Protestantism in all its forms was tolerated. Some of their neighbors and friends, members of other Separatist Churches, had already set the example. So in the year 1608 expatriation was sought to be silently effected. Owing to a law of the Crown intended to prevent subjects from going abroad, secret bargaining was made with the masters of two Dutch vessels for transportation to Holland. When upon the point of sailing, the authorities, who had been apprised of the embarkation through the perfidy of one of the Dutch masters, arrested the band of Separatists, many of whom were thrown in prison, including the leader Brewster.

Undismayed and through perseverance their efforts later were crowned with success, and by the end of the year most of the Congregation were in Amsterdam. After removing to Leyden where they remained till 1620, circumstances induced the desire to live again under the government of their native country reserving only the right of free thought and action in religious affairs.

The Congregation entered into negotiations with Sir Edwin Sandys, Treasurer of the Virginia Company that was attempting to establish a Colony in Virginia. Through his instrumentality and his friendship for Brewster arrangements were made and the first contingent set sail from Southampton in the "Mayflower" on the 5th day of August, 1620. After a tempestuous voyage the white sand cliffs of Cape Cod were rounded in the morning of Saturday, the 11th day of the following November, when at last anchor was cast in the bay on the western side of the Cape.

Other members of the Congregation embarked in following years in the "Fortune" and the "Anne".

THE MAYFLOWER PASSENGERS THEIR CHILDREN AND GRANDCHILDREN

There were 104 passengers, including men, women, and children, of whom 25 became heads of families. Two of these left only a daughter each, who married into other of the families, thus leaving 23 from whom descent is traced without duplication, as follows, viz:

JOHN ALDEN:

I — Elizabeth b. 1623 or 1624, d. May 31, 1717; m. Dec. 26, 1644 William Pabodie, b. 1620, d. Dec. 13, 1707, and had,
  1. JOHN, b. Oct. 4, 1645; d. unm.
  2. ELIZABETH, b. April 24, 1647; m. 1666 John Rogers.
  3. MARY, b. Aug. 7, 1648; m. Edward Southworth.
  4. MERCY, b. Jan. 2, 1649; m. 1671 John Simmons.
  5. MARTHA, b. Feb. 24, 1650; m. 1st, 1677, John (or Samuel) Seabury;
    m. 2nd, William Fobes.
  6. PRISCILLA, b. 1652; d. y.
  7. PRISCILLA, b. Jan. 15, 1653-4; m. Ichabod Wiswall.
  8. SARAH, b. Aug. 7, 1656; m. 1680 John Coe.
  9. RUTH, b. June 27, 1658; m. 167—, Benjamin Bartlett.
  10. REBECCA, b. Oct. 16, 1660; m. William Southworth.
  11. HANNAH, b. Oct. 15, 1662; m. 1683, Samuel Bartlett.
  12. WILLIAM, b. Nov. 24, 1664; m. 1st, Judith ——
    m. 2nd, Mary (Morgan) Starr.
  13. LYDIA, b. April 3, 1667; m. Daniel Grinnell.

II — John, b. 1626, d. March 14, 1701-2; m. 1st, before 1659, Elizabeth ——; m. 2nd, April 1, 1660, Elizabeth (Phillips) Everill, d. 1695-6, and had,
  14. MARY, b. Dec. 17, 1659; prob. d. y.

34. SARAH, b. c. 1682; d. 1739;
m. c. 1700 Thomas Southworth.
35. JONATHAN, b. March 1686;
m. 1st., Jan. 17, 1718, Elizabeth (Arnold) Waterman;
m. 2nd, prob. Mehitabel Allen.
36. ANDREW, b. ——;
m. Lydia Stanford.
37. A daughter, b.——;
perhaps m. a Simmons.

VI — Ruth, b. 1634-5, d. Oct. 12, 1674;
m. Feb. 3, 1657-8, as his first wife, John Bass, b. about 1632, d. Sept. 12, 1716, (he m. 2nd Mrs. Hannah Sturtevant) and had,
38. JOHN, b. Nov. 26, 1658;
m. 1st, Abigail Adams;
m. 2nd, Rebecca Savill.
39. SAMUEL, b. March 25, 1660;
m. 1st, Mercy Marsh;
m. 2nd, Mary Adams;
m. 3rd, Bethiah Nightingale.
40. RUTH, b. Jan. 28, 1662-3;
m. Peter Webb.
41. JOSEPH, b. Dec. 5, 1665;
m. 1st 1688, Mary Belcher;
m. 2nd, Lois Rogers.
42. HANNAH, b. June 22, 1667;
d. 24 Oct, 1705;
m. Joseph Adams; b. 24 Oct., 1654.
43. MARY, b. Feb. 11, 1669-70;
m. 1st, Christopher Webb;
m. 2nd, William Copeland.
44. SARAH, b. March 29, 1672;
m. 1692, Ephraim Thayer.

VII — Zachariah, b. about 1641. Probably a son of John Alden.
45. ANNA, b. ——; d. 1705.
m. 1699 Josiah Snell, d. 1753.
46. ZACHARIAH, b. ——;
47. JOHN (uncertain).

VIII — Mary, b. 1643, d. before Oct. 24, 1699; m., 1667, Thomas Delano, b. March 21, 1642, d. between Oct. 5, 1722 and April 22, 1723, and had,
48. BENONI, b. Oct. 30, 1667.
49. THOMAS, b. ——;
m. Hannah Bartlett.

50. JONATHAN, b. 1676;
    m. Hannah Doty.
51. DAVID ,bapt. 1678;
    m. Elizabeth Eddy.
52. MARY, (was living in 1722).
53. SARAH, b. ——;
    m. John Drew.
54. RUTH, b. ——;
    m. Samuel Drew.
55. JOSEPH, b. Sept. 1, 1685;
    m. Hannah ——.

IX— David, b. 1646, d. before May 20, 1719; m. not later than 1670, Mary dau. of Constant, Southworth, and had,
56. HENRY, b. about 1671;
    m. Deborah (perhaps Streeter)
57. RUTH, b. c. 1674; d. 1758;
    m. Samuel Sprague; d. 1740.
58. ELIZABETH, b. about 1677;
    m. John Seabury.
59. PRISCILLA, b. 1679;
    m. Samuel Cheesebrough.
60. BENJAMIN, b. ——;
    m. Hannah Brewster.
61. ALICE, b. c. 1685;
    m. 1706 Judah Paddock.
62. SAMUEL, b. c. 1689; d. Feb 24, 1781;
    m. 1728 Sarah Sprague; d. aet 70 in 1773.

* * * * * * *

ISAAC ALLERTON:

I — Remember, b. 1614; m. before Ma. 6, 1635, Moses Maverick, who d. (after having m. 2nd Mrs. Eunice Roberts) January 28, 1685-6, and had,
1. REBECCA, bap. Aug. 7, 1639;
   m. John Hawks.
2. MARY, bap. Feb. 14, 1641;
   d. ae. 15.
3. ABIGAIL, bap. Jan. 12, 1645;
   m. Samuel Ward.
4. ELIZABETH, bap. Dec. 3, 1646; d. y.
5. SAMUEL, bap. Dec. 19, 1647.

6. ELIZABETH, bap. Sept. 30, 1649;
m. 1st, Nathaniel Grafton,
m. 2nd, Thomas Skinner.
7. REMEMBER, b. Sept. 12, 1652; m. Edward Woodman.

II — Mary, b. June 1616, d. Dec. 8, 1699; m. in 1635 or 1636 Thomas Cushman; b. Feb. 1608, d. Dec. 1691, and had,
8. THOMAS, b. Sept. 16, 1637;
m. 1st, Ruth Howland,
m. 2nd, Abigail Fuller.
9. SARAH, b. ——;
m. John Hawks (his first wife was her cousin, Rebecca Maverick, q. v.)
10. LYDIA, b. ——;
m. William Harlow.
11. ISAAC, b. Feb. 8, 1647-8;
m. Rebecca Rickard.
12. ELKANAH, b. June 1, 1651;
m. 1st, Elizabeth Cole,
m. 2nd, Martha Cooke.
13. FEAR, b. June 20, 1653; d. y.
14. ELEAZER, b. Feb. 20, 1656-7;
m. Elizabeth Coombs.
15. MARY, b. ——;
m. —— Hutchinson.

III — Isaac, b. about 1630, d. 1702; m. 1st, about 1652, Elizabeth ——, d. about 1660; m. 2nd, Elizabeth (Willoughby) Colclough, about 1663, and had,
16. ELIZABETH, b. Sept. 27, 1653; m. 1st, Benjamin Starr, m. 2nd, Simon Eyres.
17. ISAAC, b. June 11, 1655; m.
18. SARAH, b. about 1670;
m. Hancock Lee.
10. A daughter, b. ——;
m. —— Newton, of Va.
20. FRANCES, b. ——;
m. Samuel Travers.
21. WILLOUGHBY, b. ——;
m. Hannah Keene (Bushrod.)

IV — BARTHOLOMEW, m. and living in England 1650; issue.

* * * * * * *

JOHN BILLINGTON:
I — Francis, b. about 1606, d. Dec. 3, 1684; m. July, 1634, Christian (Penn) widow of Francis Eaton, The Pilgrim, d. July, 1684, and had,
  1. MARTHA, b. ——;
     m. Jan. 10, 1660, Samuel Eaton.
  2. ELIZABETH, b. ——;
     m. Richard Bullock.
  3. REBECCA, b. June 8, 1647.
  4. MARY, b. ——;
     m. Samuel Sabin.
  5. ISAAC, b. ——;
     m. Hannah Glass.
  6. MERCY, b. ——;
     m. John Martin.
  7. DESIRE, b. ——;
  8. JOSEPH, b. ——;
  9. FRANCIS, b. ——;
     m. Abigail Churchill.

* * * * * *

WILLIAM BRADFORD:
I — William, b. June 17, 1624, d. Feb. 20, 1703-4; m. 1st, Alice, dau. of Thomas Richards, b. 1627, d. Dec. 12, 1671; m. 2nd, Mrs. —— Wiswall; m. 3rd, Mrs. Mary Holmes, d. Jan. 6, 1714-15.
Children by first wife.
  1. JOHN, b. Feb. 20, 1651-2;
     m. Mercy Warren.
  2. WILLIAM, b. March 11, 1654-5;
     m. Rebecca Bartlett.
  3. THOMAS, b. about 1656;
     m. Ann Smith.
  4. ALICE, b. about 1658;
     m. 1st, William Adams,
     m. 2nd, James Fitch.
  5. MERCY, b. Sept. 2, 1660;
     m. Samuel Steele.
  6. HANNAH, b. May 9, 1662;
     m. Josiah Ripley.
  7. MELATIAH, b. about 1664;
     m. 1st, John Steele,
     m. 2nd, Samuel Stevens.
  8. SAMUEL, b. ——, 1668;
     m. Hannah Rogers.

    9. MARY, bapt. 1669;
       m. William Hunt.
   10. SARAH, b. ——, 1671;
       m. Kenelm Baker.
Child by second wife,
   11. JOSEPH, b. 1674;
       m. 1st, Anna Fitch,
       m. 2nd, Mrs. Mary Fitch.
Children by third wife,
   12. ISRAEL, b. about 1678;
       m. Sarah Bartlett.
   13. EPHRAIM, b. 1680;
       m. Elizabeth Brewster.
   14. DAVID, b. ——;
       m. Elizabeth Finney.
   15. HEZEKIAH, b. ——;
       m. Mary Chandler.

II — Joseph, b. about 1630, d. July 10, 1715; m. May 25, 1664, Jael, dau. of Peter Hobart, bapt. Dec. 30, 1643, d. April 14, 1730, and had,
   16. ELISHA, b. ——;
       m. 1st, Hannah Cole,
       m. 2nd, Bathsheba LaBrocke.
   17. JOSEPH, b. ——;

III — MERCY, m. Benj. Vermayes.

    * * * * * * * *

WILLIAM BREWSTER:

I — Jonathan, b. Aug. 12, 1593, d. Aug. 7, 1659; m. April 10, 1624, Lucretia Oldham, d. March 4, 1678-9, and had,
    1. WILLIAM, b. March 9, 1625; probably went to England.
    2. MARY, b. April 16, 1627;
       m. John Turner
    3. JONATHAN, b. July 17, 1629; probably went to England.
    4. RUTH, b. Oct. 3, 1631;
       m. 1st, John Pickett,
       m. 2nd, Charles Hill.
    5. BENJAMIN, b. Nov. 17, 1633;
       m. Anne Dart.
    6. ELIZABETH, b. May 1, 1637;
       m. 1st, Peter Bradley,
       m. 2nd, Christopher Christophers.
    7. GRACE, b. Nov. 1, 1639;
       m. Daniel Wetherell.

  8. HANNAH, b. Nov. 3, 1641;
   m. Samuel Starr.
II — Patience, d. 1634; m. Aug. 5, 1624
Thomas Prence, d. March 29, 1673,
and had,
  9. THOMAS, b. ——;
   went to England.
  10. REBECCA, b. ——;
   m. Edmond Freeman.
  11. HANNAH, b. ——;
   m. 1st, Nathaniel Mayo,
   m. 2nd, Jonathan Sparrow.
  12. MERCY, b. ——;
   m. John Freeman.
III — Fear, d. Dec. 12, 1634; m. as his
second wife, Isaac Allerton, The
Pilgrim, and had,
  ISAAC, b. about 1630.
  (Issue; see Allerton famliy.)
IV — Love, d. 1650-51; m. May 15, 1634,
Sarah Collier, d. April 26, 1691,
and had,
  13. SARAH, b. ——;
   m. Benjamin Bartlett.
  14. NATHANIEL, b. ——;
   m. Sarah (prob. North).
  15. WILLIAM, b. ——;
   m. Lydia Partridge.
  16. WRESTLING, b. ——;
   m. Mary ——.
V — WRESTLING, d. unm.

   * * * * * * * *

PETER BROWN:

I — Mary, m. Ephraim Tinkham; he d.
between Jan. 17, 1683 and May 20,
1685, and had,
  1. EPHRAIM, b. Aug. 5, 1649;
   m. Esther Wright.
  2. EBENEZER, b. Sept. 30, 1651;
   m. Elizabeth Burroughs.
  3. PETER, b. Dec. 25, 1653;
   m. Mercy Mendhall.
  4. HEZEKIAH, b. Feb. 8, 1655-6;
   m. Ruth ——.
  5. JOHN, m. June 7, 1658; d. y.
  6. MARY, b. Aug. 5, 1661;
   m. John Thompson.
  7. JOHN, b. Nov. 15, 1663;
   m. Sarah ——.

8. ISAAC, b. April 11, 1666;
      m. Sarah King.

II — Rebecca, m. William Snow, and had
   9. WILLIAM, b. ——;
      m. Naomi Whitman.
   10. JAMES, b. ——; d. 1690.
   11. JOSEPH, b. ——;
      m. Hopestill Alden.
   12. BENJAMIN, b. ——;
      m. 1st, Elizabeth Alden,
      m. 2nd, Sarah (Allen) Cary.
   13. MARY, b. ——;
   14. LYDIA, b. ——;
   15. HANNAH, b. ——;
      m. Giles Rickard.
   16. REBECCA, b. ——;
      m. Samuel Rickard.

III — PRISCILLA, m. William Allen.

* * * * * * * *

JAMES CHILTON:

I — Mary, d. 1679; m. Oct. 12, 1624, John Winslow, b. April 16, 1597, d. 1674, and had,
   1. SUSANNA, b. ——;
      m. Robert Latham.
   2. MARY, b. ——;
      m. Edward Gray.
   3. EDWARD, b. ——;
      m. 1st, Sarah Hilton,
      m. 2nd, Elizabeth Hutchinson.
   4. SARAH, b. ——;
      m. 1st, Miles Standish,
      m. 2nd, Tobias Payne,
      m. 3rd, Richard Middlecot.
   5. JOHN, b. ——;
      m. 1st, Elizabeth ——;
      m. 2nd, Judith ——.
   6. JOSEPH, b. ——;
      m. Sarah Lawrence.
   7. SAMUEL, b. ——;
      m. Hannah Briggs.
   8. ISAAC, b. ——;
      m. Mary Nowell.
   9. ANNE, b. ——;
      m. —— LeBlond.
   10. BENJAMIN, b. Aug. 12, 1653;
      prob. d. y.

II — Isabella, m. July 21, 1615, Roger Chandler, in Holland. Said to have settled in Duxbury.

* * * * * * * *

FRANCIS COOKE:

I — John, d. Nov. 23, 1695; m. July 6, 1634, Sarah, dau. of Richard Warren, The Pilgrim, and had,
1. SARAH, b. —— 1635; m. Arthur Hathaway.
2. JOHN, b. ——.
3. ELIZABETH, b. ——; m. Daniel Wilcox.
4. ESTHER, b. Aug. 16, 1650; m. Thomas Taber.
5. MARY, b. Jan. 12, 1652; m. Philip Taber.
6. MERCY, b. July 25, 1655; m. Stephen West.

II — Jacob, b. about 1618, d. Dec. 1675; m. 1st, Damaris, dau. of Stephen Hopkins, the Pilgrim, 1646; m. 2nd, Elizabeth (Lettice) Shurtleff, Nov. 18, 1669, and had,
7. ELIZABETH, b. Jan. 18, 1648-9; m. John Doty.
8. CALEB, b. March 29, 1651; m. Jane ——.
9. JACOB, b. March 23, 1653; m. Lydia Miller.
10. MARY, b. Jan. 12, 1657-8; m. John Rickard.
11. MARTHA, b. March 16, 1659-60; m. Elkanah Cushman.
12. FRANCIS, b. Jan. 5, 1662-3; m. Elizabeth Latham.
13. RUTH, b. Jan. 17, 1665-6.
14. SARAH, b. —— 1670 or 1671; m. Robert Bartlett.

III — Hester, m. Nov. 21, 1644, Richard Wright who d. June 9, 1691, and had,
15. ADAM, b. about 1645; m. 1st, Sarah Soule, m. 2nd, Mehitabel Barrows.
16. ESTHER, b. 1649; m. Ephraim Tinkham.

17. MARY, m. —— Price.
18. JOHN, prob. d. y.
19. Isaac, prob .d. y.

IV — Jane, d. prior to June 8, 1666; m. 1627 or 1628, Experience Mitchell, d. 1689, and had,
20. ELIZABETH, m. John Washburn.
21. THOMAS, prob d. y.
22. MARY, m. James Shaw.
23. EDWARD, m. 1st, Mary Hayward, m. 2nd, Alice Bradford.
24. SARAH, m. John Hayward.
25. JACOB, b. 1645;
m. Susannah Pope.
26. JOHN, m. 1st, Mary Bonney,
m. 2nd, Mary Lothrop,
m. 3rd, Mary Prior.
27. HANNAH, m. Joseph Hayward.

V — Mary, b. 1624; d. March 21, 1714; m. Dec. 26, 1643, John Thompson, d. June 16, 1696, and had,
28. ADAM, b. ——; d. y.
29. JOHN, b. Nov. 24, 1649;
m. Mary Tinkham.
30. MARY, b. ——;
m. Thomas Taber.
31. ESTHER, b. July 28, 1652;
m. William Reed.
32. ELIZABETH, b. Jan. 28, 1654;
m. William Swift.
38. SARAH, b. April 7, 1657.
34. LYDIA, b. Oct. 5, 1659;
m. James Soule.
35. JACOB, b. April 24, 1662;
m. Abigail Wadsworth.
36. THOMAS, b. Oct. 19, 1664;
m. Mary Morton.
37. PETER, b. ——;
m. Sarah Wood.
38. MERCY, b. ——, 1671;
d. April 19, 1756, unm.

* * * * * * * *

EDWARD DOTY:

I — Edward, d. Feb. 8, 1689-90; m. Feb. 25, 1662-3, Sarah Faunce, (she m. 2nd April 26, 1693, John Buck, and d. June 27, 1695), and had,

1. EDWARD, b. May 20, 1664; prob. d. between 1690 and 1696.
2. SARAH, b. June 9, 1666; m. 1st, James Warren, m. 2nd, John Bacon.
3. JOHN, b. Aug. 4, 1668; drowned Feb. 8, 1689-90.
4. MARTHA, b. July 9, 1671; m. Thomas Morton.
5. MARY, b. July 9, 1671; m. Joseph Allyn.
6. ELIZABETH, b. Dec. 22, 1673; m. Tobias Oakman.
7. PATIENCE, b. July 7, 1676; d. Feb. 28, 1690-91.
8. MERCY, b. Feb. 6, 1678; d. Nov. 30, 1682.
9. SAMUEL, b. May 17, 1681; m. Anne Buckingham.
10. MERCY, b. Sept. 23, 1684; m. Daniel Pratt.
11. BENJAMIN, b. May 30, 1689. m. Hester Bemen.

II — John, d. May 8, 1701; m. 1667, Elizabeth Cooke, b. Jan. 18, 1648-9, d. Nov. 21, 1692; m. 2nd Sarah Jones, and had,

12. JOHN, b. August 24, 1668; m. 1st, Mehitabel Nelson, m. 2nd, Hannah Sherman.
13. EDWARD, b. June 28, 1671; prob. d. y.
14. JACOB, b. May 27, 1673; prob. d. y.
15. ELIZABETH, b. Feb. 10, 1675-6; m. Joshua Morse.
16. ISAAC, b. Oct. 25, 1678; m. Martha Faunce.
17. SAMUEL, b. Jan. 31, 1682-3; m. Mercy Cobb.
18. ELISHA, b. July 13, 1686; m. Hannah ———.

19. JOSIAH, b. Oct. 1689;
    m. Abigail ——.
20. MARTHA, b. Oct. 1692;
    m. Ebenezer Curtis.
21. SARAH, b. Feb. 19, 1695-6.
22. PATIENCE, b. July 3, 1697;
    m. Kenelm Baker.
23. DESIRE, b. April 19, 1699;
    m. George Barrows.

III — Thomas, d. 1679; m. 1st Mary Churchill, m. 2nd Mary ——, and had,
24. MARTHA, b. ——, 1672.
25. HANNAH, b. Dec. 1675;
    m. Jonathan Delano.
26. THOMAS, b. July 22, 1679;
    m. 1st, Elizabeth Harlow,
    m. 2nd, Mercy Ellis.

IV — Samuel, d. 1715; m. Nov. 15, 1678, Jane Harmon, and had,
27. SAMUEL, b. Aug. 27, 1679;
    m. Elizabeth Hull.
28. SARAH, b. March 2, 1681.
29. JOHN, b. ——; (uncertain).
30. ISAAC, b. Aug. 12, 1682;
    m. Frances ——.
31. EDWARD, b. May 14, 1685;
    m. Sarah ——.
32. JAMES, b. Sept. 17, 1686;
    m. Phebe Slater.
33. JONATHAN, b. Feb. 24, 1687-8; m. Mary ——.
34. BENJAMIN, b. May 14, 1691;
    prob. m. Abigail Whitehead.
35. ELIZABETH, b. Feb. 26, 1695;
    m. David Martin.
36. JOSEPH, b. Oct. 30, 1696;
    m. Sarah Badgly.
37. DANIEL, b. March 9, 1701-2.
38. MARGARET, b. March 5, 1704-5.
39. NATHANIEL, b. prob. about 1707-8; m. ——.

V — Desire, d. Jan. 1731; m. 1st, Dec. 25, 1667, William Sherman, b. about 1644, d. Oct. 25, 1679; m. 2nd, Nov. 24, 1681, Israel Holmes, d. Feb. 24, 1684-5; m. 3rd, Alexander Standish, and had

40. HANNAH SHERMAN, b. Feb. 21, 1668; m. William Ring.
41. ELIZABETH SHERMAN, b. March 11, 1670; d. 1695; prob. unm.
42. WILLIAM SHERMAN, b. April 19, 1672; m. Mary White.
43. PATIENCE SHERMAN, b. Aug. 3, 1674.
44. EXPERIENCE SHERMAN, b. Sept. 22, 1678; m. Miles Standish.
45. EBENEZER SHERMAN, b. April 21, 1680; m. 1st, Margaret Decrow; m. 2nd, Bathsheba Ford.
46. ISRAEL HOLMES, b. Feb. 17, 1682-3; m. Elizabeth Turner.
47. JOHN HOLMES, b. Jan. 15, 1684-5; m. 1st, Joanna Sprague; M. 2nd, Sarah Thomas.
48. DESIRE STANDISH, b. May 5, 1689; m. Nathan Weston.
49. THOMAS STANDISH, b. Jan. 29, 1690; m. Mary Carver.
50. ICHABOD STANDISH, b. June 10, 1693; m. Phebe Ring.

VI — Elizabeth, m. Jan. 13, 1674-5, John Rouse b. 1643, d. Oct., 1717, and had,
51. JOHN, b. ——, 1678; d. May 26, 1704.

VII — Isaac, m. Elizabeth England, and had,
52. ISAAC, b. about 1672; m. Elizabeth Jackson.
53. JOSEPH, b. about 1680; m. Sarah ——.
54. JACOB, b. about 1682; m. Penelope Albertson.
55. SOLOMON, b. about 1691; m. Rachel Seaman.
56. JAMES, b. Dec. 21, 1693; m. Catherine Latting.
57. SAMUEL, b. about 1695; m. Charity Mudge.

VIII — Joseph, d. about 1732-5; m. 1st, probably Deborah Ellis (?)

d. June 21, 1711; m. 2nd, March 9,
1712, Sarah Edwards. He had,
58. THEOPHILUS, b. 1674;
m. Ruth Mendall (?)
59. ELIZABETH, b. 1678-9;
m. John Lewis.
60. ELLIS, b. 1681;
m. Elinor ——.
61. JOSEPH, b. March 31, 1683;
m. Hannah Edwards.
62. DEBORAH, b. March 31, 1685;
m. Joseph Landers.
63. JOHN, b. March 1, 1688;
m. Elizabeth ——.
64. MERCY, b. Jan. 12, 1691.
65. FAITH, b. Jan. 18, 1696;
m. Jonathan Shaw.
66. MARY, b. July 28, 1699;
m. Samuel Waterman.

IX — Mary, m. Samuel Hatch, b. Dec.
22, 1653, d. about 1735, and had,
67. SAMUEL, b. Nov. 10, 1678;
m. Elizabeth Oldham.
68. JOSIAH, b. May 30, 1680;
m. Desire Hawes.
69. HANNAH, b. Feb. 15, 1681-2.
70. EBENEZER, b. April 6, 1684;
m. ——.
71. ISAAC, b. Dec. 20, 1687;
m.——.
72. ELIZABETH, b. June 16, 1690;
m. John Bonney.
73. ELISHA, b. Nov. 7, 1692;
m. Patience Keen.
74. EZEKIEL, b. May 14, 1695;
m. Ruth Church.
75. DESIRE, b. Sept. 25, 1698;
prob. m. Joseph Lovell.

FRANCIS EATON:
I — Samuel, d. about 1684; m. 1st,
Elizabeth ——; m. 2nd, Jan. 10,
1660, Martha Billington, and had,
6. SARAH, b. ——;
m. Philip Bumpas.
2. MERCY, b. ——;
m. Samuel Fuller.
3. SAMUEL, b. ——;
m. Elizabeth Fuller.

II — Rachel, m. March 2, 1645, Joseph
(or Daniel) Ramsden, d. May 25,
1674, and had,
4. DANIEL, b. Sept. 14, 1649,
III — Benjamin, d. Jan. 16, 1711-12;
m. Dec. 4, 1660, Sarah Hoskins.
b. Sept. 16, 1636, and had,
5. WILLIAM, b. ——; no issue.
6. BENJAMIN, b. 1664;
m. 1st, Mary Coombs,
m. 2nd, Susanna Beal.
7. REBECCA, b. ——;
m. Josiah Rickard.
8. EBENEZER, b.——;
m. Hannah Rickard.

* * * * * *

EDWARD FULLER:
I — Samuel, d. Oct. 31, 1683; m. April
8, 1635, Jane Lothrop b. 1614, who
d. before her husband, and had,
1. HANNAH, b. ——;
m. Nicholas Bonham.
2. SAMUEL, bapt. Feb. 11, 1637-
8, m. Anne Fuller.
3. ELIZABETH, b. ——;
m. Joseph (?) Taylor.
4. SARAH, bapt. Aug. 1, 1641;
d. y.
5. MARY, b. June 16, 1644;
m. Joseph Williams.
6. THOMAS, b. March 18, 1651;
d. y.
7. SARAH, b. Dec. 10, 1654;
m. John Crowell.
8. JOHN, b. about 1656;
m. Mehitabel Rowley.
9. A child, b. Feb. 8, 1658; d. y.

* * * * * *

SAMUEL FULLER:
I — Samuel, d. Aug. 17, 1695; m. Elizabeth ——; m. 2nd, Elizabeth, widow
of Thos. Bowen, and had,
1. MERCY, b. ——;
m. Daniel Cole.
2. SAMUEL, b. 1659;
m. Mercy Eaton.
3. EXPERIENCE, b. about 1661;
m. James Wood.

4. JOHN, b. 1663;
   m. Mercy Nelson.
5. ELIZABETH, b. 1666;
   m. Samuel Eaton.
6. HANNAH, b. 1668;
   m. Eleazer Lewis.
7. ISAAC, b. 1675;
   m. Mary Pratt.

* * * * * * *

STEPHEN HOPKINS:

I — Giles, d. about 1690; m. Oct. 9, 1639, Catherine Wheldon, and had,
  1. MARY, b. Nov. 1640;
     m. Samuel Smith.
  2. STEPHEN, b. Sept. 1642;
     m. 1st, Mary Merrick;
     m. 2nd, Bethiah Atkins.
  3. JOHN, b. 1643; d. y.
  4. ABIGAIL, b. Oct. 1644;
     m. William Merrick.
  5. DEBORAH, b. June, 1648;
     m. Josiah Cooke.
  6. CALEB, b. Jan. 1650-1;
     m. Mary Williams.
  7. RUTH, b. June, 1653;
     m. Samuel Mayo.
  8. JOSHUA, b. June, 1657;
     m. Mary Cole.
  9. WILLIAM, b. Jan. 9, 1660-1;
     d. unm.
  10. ELIZABETH, b. Nov. 1664;
     d. y.

II — Constance, d. Oct. 1677; m. 1627, Nicholas Snow, d. Nov. 15, 1676, and had,
  11. MARK, b. May 9, 1628;
     m. 1st, Anna Cooke;
     m. 2nd, Jane Prence.
  12. MARY, b. about 1630;
     m. Thomas Paine.
  13. SARAH, b. about 1632;
     m. William Walker.
  14. JOSEPH, b. about 1634;
     m. Mary ———.
  15. SEPHEN, b. about 1636;
     m. 1st, Susanna (Deane) Rogers, m. 2nd, Mary Bigford.
  16. JOHN, b. about 1638;
     m. Mary Walden.

17. ELIZABETH, b. about 1640; m. Thomas Rogers.
18. JABEZ, b. about 1642; m. Elizabeth Smith.
19. RUTH, b. about 1644; m. John Cole.
20. A child; no further record.

III — Damaris, m. Jacob Cooke. (Issue; see Cooke family).

IV — Deborah, m. April 23, 1646, Andrew Ring, d. Feb. 22, 1693-4, and had,
21. ELIZABETH, b. April 19, 1652; m. William Mayo.
22. WILLIAM, b. 1653; m. Hannah Sherman.
23. ELEAZER, b. ——; m. Mary Shaw.
24. MARY, b. ——; m. John Morton.
25. DEBORAH.
26. SUSANNA.
27. SAMUEL, b. ——, (Not named in father's will.)

* * * * * *

JOHN HOWLAND:

I — Desire, d. Dec. 13, 1683; m. 1643, John Gorham d. Feb. 5, 1676, and had,
1. DESIRE, b. April 2, 1644; m. John Hawes.
2. TEMPERANCE, b. May 5, 1646; m. 1st, Edward Sturgis, m. 2nd, Thomas Baxter.
3. ELIZABETH, b. April 2, 1648; m. Joseph Hallett.
4. JAMES, b. April 28, 1650; m. Hannah Huckins.
5. JOHN, b. Feb. 20, 1652; m. Mary Otis.
6. JOSEPH, b. Feb. 16, 1654; m. Sarah Sturgis.
7. JABEZ, b. Aug. 3, 1656; m. Hannah (Sturgis) Gray.
8. MERCY, b. Jan. 20, 1658; m. George Denison.
9. LYDIA, b. Nov. 16, 1661; m. John Thacher.

10. HANNAH, b. Nov. 28, 1663;
m. Joseph Whelden.
11. SHUBAEL, b. Oct. 21, 1667;
m. Puella Hussey.

II — John, m. Dec. 26, 1651, Mary Lee, and had,
12. MARY, b. 1653;
m. John Allyn.
13. ELIZABETH, b. May 17, 1655;
m. John Bursley.
14. ISAAC, b. Nov. 25, 1659;
m. Ann Taylor.
15. HANNAH, b. May 15, 1661;
m. Jonathan Crocker.
16. MERCY, b. Jan. 21, 1663;
m. Joseph Hamlin.
17. LYDIA, b. Jan. 9, 1665;
m. Joseph Jenkins.
18. EXPERIENCE, b. July 28, 1668.
19. ANNE, b. Sept. 9, 1670;
m. Joseph Crocker.
20. SHUBAEL, b. Sept. 30, 1672;
m. Mercy Blossom.
21. JOHN, b. Dec. 31, 1674;
m. 1st, Abigail Crocker,
m. 2nd, Mary Crocker.

III — Jabez, d. between May 14, 1708 and Feb. 21, 1712; m. Bethiah Thacher, d. Dec. 19, 1725, and had,
22. JABEZ, b. Nov. 15, 1669;
m. Patience Stafford.
23. JOHN, b. Jan. 15, 1673; d. y.
24. BETHIAH, b. June 3, 1674;
d. 1676.
25. JOSIAH, b. Aug. 6, 1676;
m. Yetmercy Shove.
26. JOHN, b. July 26, 1679;
prob. d. unmarried.
27. JUDAH, b. May 7, 1683; d. y.
28. SETH, b. Jan 5, 1685; d. y.
29. SAMUEL, b. May 16, 1686;
m. 1st, Abigail Cary,
m. 2nd, prob. Mrs. Rachel Allen.
30. EXPERIENCE, b. May 19, 1687; d. y.
31. JOSEPH, b. Oct. 14, 1692;
m. Bathsheba Cary.

32. ELIZABETH, b. ——;
    m. Nathan Townsend.

IV — Hope, d. Jan. 8, 1683; m. 1646 John
    Chipman, b. about 1614, d. April 7,
    1708, and had,
33. ELIZABETH, b. June 24, 1647;
    m. Hosea Joyce.
34. HOPE, b. Aug. 31, 1652;
    m. 1st, John Huckins,
    m. 2nd, Jonathan Cobb.
35. LYDIA, b. Dec. 25, 1654;
    m. John Sargent.
36. JOHN, b. March 2, 1657; d. y.
37. HANNAH, b. Jan. 14, 1659;
    m. Thomas Huckins.
38. SAMUEL, b. April 15, 1661;
    m. Sarah Cobb.
39. RUTH, b. Dec. 31, 1662;
    m. Eleazer Crocker.
40. BETHIAH, b. July 1, 1666;
    m. Shubael Dimock.
41. MERCY, b. Feb. 6, 1668;
    m. Nathan Skiff.
42. JOHN, b. March 3, 1671;
    m. 1st, Mary Skiff,
    m. 2nd, Elizabeth (Handley)
        Russell,
    m. 3rd, Hannah Hoxie.
43. DESIRE, b. Feb. 26, 1674;
    m. Melatiah Bourne.

V — Lydia, m. James Brown, d. Oct. 29,
    1710, and had,
44. JAMES, b. May 4, 1655;
    m. Margaret Denison.
45. DOROTHY, b. Aug. 29, 1666;
    m. Joseph Kent.
46. JABEZ, b. July 9, 1668;
    m. Jane ——.

VI — Ruth, m. Nov. 17, 1664, Thomas
    Cushman, b. Sept. 16, 1637, d. Aug.
    23, 1726, and had,
47. ROBERT, b. Oct. 4, 1665;
    m. 1st, Persis ——,
    m. 2nd, Prudence Sherman.
48. DESIRE, b. 1668;
    prob. m. Samuel Kent.

VII — Hannah, m. July 6, 1661, Jonathan
    Bosworth, and had,
49. MERCY, b. May 30, 1662.

50. HANNAH, b. Nov. 5, 1663;
m. Nathaniel Jenks.
51. JONATHAN, b. Dec. 24, 1666;
d. 1673.
52. DAVID, b. Sept. 15, 1670;
m. Mary Sturtevant.
53. ELIZABETH, b. June 6, 1665;
d. 1676.
54. JOHN, b. April 6, 1671;
m. Elizabeth Toogood.
55. JABEZ, b. Feb. 14, 1673.
56. ICHABOD, b. March 18, 1676;
m. Sarah Stacy.
57. JONATHAN, b. Sept. 22, 1680;
m. Sarah Rounds.

VIII — Joseph, m. Dec. 7, 1664, Elizabeth Southworth, and had,
58. LYDIA, b. ——, 1665;
m. Jeremiah Thomas.
59. ELIZABETH, b. ——;
m. 1st, Isaac Hamlin,
m. 2nd, Timothy Cannon.
60. MARY, b. ——;
m. George Conant.
61. THOMAS, b. ——;
m. Joanna Cole.
62. JAMES, b. ——;
m. Mary Lothrop.
63. NATHANIEL, b. ——;
m. 1st, Martha Cole,
m. 2nd, Abigail (Churchill)
Billington.
64. SARAH, b. 1687.
65. BENJAMIN, b. 1689; d. y.
66. JOSEPH, b. ——; d. y.

IX — Isaac, d. March 9, 1724; m. Elizabeth Vaughn, b. 1652, d. Oct. 29, 1727, and had,
67. SETH, b. Nov. 28, 1677;
m. Elizabeth Delano.
68. ISAAC, b. March 6, 1679;
m. Sarah Thomas.
69. PRISCILLA, b. Aug. 22, 1681;
m. Peter Bennett.
70. ELIZABETH, b. 1682: d. y.
71. NATHAN, b. Jan. 17, 1687;
m. Frances Coombs.
72. JAEL, b. Oct. 13, 1688;
m. Nathaniel Southworth.

73. SUSANNAH, b. Oct. 14, 1690;
m. Ephraim Wood.
74. HANNAH, b. Oct. 16, 1694;
m. John Tinkham.
X — Elizabeth, b. ——; d. ——;
m. 1st, Ephraim Hicks;
m. 2nd, John Dickenson.

* * * * * * *

RICHARD MORE:
I — Caleb, b. c. 1644; d. Jan. 1678-9;
probably unm.
II — Richard, m. Sarah ——, and had,
1. SAMUEL, d. y.
Others.
III — Susanna, b. 1650, living in Oct., 1728;
m. 1st, Samuel Dutch; d. ante. 1693;
m. 2nd, Richard Hutton; d. ante. 1714;
m. 3rd, 1714, John Knowlton, Sr.;
Children by her first husband,
1. BARBARA, d. y.
2. SUSANNA, married Benjamin Knowlton.
IV — Christian, b. 1652, d. May 30, 1680;
m. (first wife) Joshua Conant.
1. JOSHUA, b. May 12, 1678.

* * * * * * *

DEGORY PRIEST:
I — Mary, d. about 1689; m. 1630 Phineas Pratt, d. April 19, 1680, and had,
1. JOHN, m. Ann Barker.
2. SAMUEL, m. Mary Barker.
3. DANIEL.
4. PETER.
5. JOSEPH, m. Dorcas Folger.
6. AARON, b. about 1654;
m. 1st, Sarah Pratt,
m. 2nd, Sarah (Wright) Cummings.
7. MARY, m. John Swann. (?)
8. MERCY.
II — Sarah, m. John Coombs, and had,
9. FRANCIS,
m. 1st, Deborah Morton,
m. 2nd, Mary (Barker) Pratt.

* * * * * * *

THOMAS ROGERS:

I — Joseph, d. 1678; m. Hannah ———, and had,
1. SARAH, b. Aug. 6, 1633; d. y.
2. JOSEPH, b. July 19, 1635; m. Susannah Deane.
3. THOMAS, b. March 29, 1638; m. Elizabeth Snow.
4. ELIZABETH, b. Sept. 29, 1639; m. Jonathan Higgins.
5. JOHN, b. April 3, 1642; m. Elizabeth Twining.
6. MARY, b. Sept. 22, 1644; m. John Finney.
7. JAMES, b. Oct. 18, 1648; m. Mary Paine.
8. HANNAH, b. Aug. 8, 1652.

II — John, d. between Aug. 26, 1691, and Sept. 20, 1692; m. April 16, 1639, Ann Churchman, and had,
9. JOHN, b. 1640;
   m. 1st, Elizabeth Pabodie,
   m. 2nd, Hannah (Hobart) Brown.
10. ABIGAIL, b. 1641-2; m. John Richmond.
11. ANNA, m. 1st, John Tisdale,
    m. 2nd, Thomas Terry,
    m. 3rd, Samuel Williams.
12. ELIZABETH, m. Nathaniel Williams.

* * * * * * *

HENRY SAMPSON:

I — Elizabeth, m. Robert Sproat, d. between Nov. 23, 1711, and Dec. 11, 1712, and had,
1. MERCY, b. July 15, 1662; m. Thomas Oldham.
2. ELIZABETH, b. July 1664; unmarried in 1711.
3. MARY, b. May 1, 1666; unmarried in 1711.
4. ROBERT, b. April, 1669; d. 1690, unm.
5. ANNA, b. March, 1671-2; m. Ebenezer Richmond.

    6. JAMES, b. Feb., 1673-4;
       m. 1st, Elizabeth Southworth,
       m. 2nd, Rachel Dwelly.
    7. EBENEZER, b. May, 1676;
       m. Experience Hawes.
    8. HANNAH, b. Aug., 1680;
       m. Ephraim Kean.

II — Hannah, m. March 20, 1665, Josiah Holmes, and had,
    9. HANNAH, b. Oct. 11, 1667.
  10. DORCAS, b. Aug. 4, 1669.
  11. JOSIAH, b. Aug. 13, 1672.
  12. MARY, b. Nov. 5, 1674.
  13. JOHN, b. May 28, 1678;
       m. Susannah (Randall) Stetson
  14. WILLIAM, b. Jan. 18, 1679-80; m. Bathsheba Stetson.

III — Dorcas, married Thomas Bonney, and had,
  15. EBENEZER, d. Nov. 25, 1712; prob. unmarried.
  16. THOMAS, m. Sarah Studley.
  17. ELIZABETH, m. Ephraim Northcutt.
  18. MERCY, m. 1st Nathaniel Delano; m. 2nd, John Curtis.
  19. MARY, m. John Mitchell.
  20. JOSEPH, m. Margaret Phillips.
  21. JOHN, m. 1st, Elizabeth ——
       m. 2nd, Elizabeth Hatch.
  22. JAMES, m. Abigail Bishop.
  23. WILLIAM, m. 1st, Ann May, m. 2nd, Mehitabel ——.

IV — James, d. between Jan. 10, 1715-16 and July 7, 1718; m. Hannah ——, and had,
  24. JAMES, m. Ruth Sawyer.
  25. HENRY.
  26. JOSEPH; m. Sarah Sampson.
  27. ANNE, m. Shubael Smith.
  28. PENELOPE, m. Abraham Sampson.
  29. SUSANNA, m. Benjamin Hillman.
  30. PRISCILLA, m. Samuel Hammond.

V — Stephen, m. Elizabeth ——, and had,
  31. BENJAMIN, b. 1686; m. Rebecca Cooke.

  32. JOHN, b. Aug. 17, 1688; m. Priscilla Bartlett.
  33. CORNELIUS, d. prob. ante. 1724.
  34. HANNAH, m. Robert Tyler.
  35. Mary, m. Samuel Thayer.
  36. ELIZABETH, m. Jonathan Thayer.
  37. DORCAS, m. John Plumley.
  38. ABIGAIL, m. George Bruce.

VI — Caleb, m. 1st, Mercy Standish; prob. m. 2nd Jan. 3, 1728-9, Rebecca Stanford.
He had,
  39. DAVID, m. Mary Chaffin.
  40. LORA; m. Benjamin Simmons.
  41. RACHEL, m. Moses Smmions.
  42. PRISCILLA, b. 1697; d. unm.
  43. CALEB, m. Mehitabel Ford.
  44. JOSHUA, m. Mary Oakman.
  45. JERUSHA, m. Ebenezer Bartlett.
  46. RUTH, m. John Fullerton.
  47. SARAH, prob d. unm.

VII — Mary, m. John Summers.

VIII — a dau.; m. John Hanmore.

* * * * * *

GEORGE SOULE

I — Mary, m. John Peterson, d. between April 20, 1718, and March 7, 1719-20, and had,
  1. JOHN, d. 1690; prob. unm.
  2. JOSEPH, m. Mrs. Sarah Doty.
  3. BENJAMIN, m. Hannah Wadsworth.
  4. JONATHAN, m. Lydia Thacher.
  5. DAVID, b. Oct. 1, 1676; d. Sept. 30, 1760, unm.
  6. ISAAC, m. Mary Hobart.
  7. MARTHA; unm. in 1718.
  8. MARY, m. her cousin, Joseph Soule (No. 17).
  9. REBECCA, m. John Weston.

II — John, d. about 1707; m. 1st, Rebecca Simmons; m. 2nd, 1678, Esther (Nash) Sampson, b. March 6, 1639, d. Sept. 12, 1735. He had,
  10. JOHN, m. Martha Tinkham.

11. AARON, m. Mary Wadsworth.
12. MOSES, m. Mercy Southworth.
13. REBECCA, b. about 1657;
    m. Edmond Weston.
14. JAMES, b. 1659;
    m. Lydia Thompson.
15. BENJAMIN, b. 1666;
    m. Sarah Standish.
16. RACHEL, b. 1662;
    m. John Cobb.
17. JOSEPH, b. July 31, 1679;
    m. Mary Peterson (No. 8).
18. ZACHARIAH, d. unm.
19. SARAH, m. Adam Wright.
20. JOSHUA, b. Oct. 12, 1681;
    m. Joanna Studley.
21. JOSIAH, m. Lydia Delano.

III — George, d. about 1704, m. Deborah ———, and had,
22. WILLIAM, m. Hannah ———.
23. JOHN, d. May 11, 1704.
24. NATHANIEL, m. Mary ———.
25. DEBORAH, unm. in 1709.
26. MARY, m. Joseph Davoll.
27. LYDIA, m. William Brownell.
28. SARAH.
29. GEORGE, m. ———.

IV — Nathaniel, m. Rose ———, and had,
30. NATHANIEL,
    m. 1st Meribah Gifford,
    m. 2nd, Hannah Macomber.
31. SYLVANUS.
32. JACOB, m. Rebecca Gifford.
33. MILES.

V — Patience, d. March 11, 1705-6; m. Jan. 1666, John Haskell, d. May 15, 1706, and had,
34. JOHN, b. June 11, 1670;
    m. Mary Squire.
35. ELIZABETH, b. July 2, 1672;
    m. Thomas Drinkwater.
36. WILLIAM, b. June 11, 1674.
37. PATIENCE, b. Feb. 1, 1679;
    d. Feb. 14, 1705-6.
38. BETHIAH, b. Jan. 5, 1681.
39. MARY, b. July 4, 1684;
    m. Scottoway Clark.

    40. JOSIAH, b. June 18, 1686;
        m. 1st, Sarah Kennedy,
        m. 2nd, Sarah Brayley.
    41. SUSANNAH, b. Jan. 15, 1691.
VI — Elizabeth, m. Francis Walker.

* * * * * *

MYLES STANDISH:

I — Alexander, d. July 6, 1702; m. 1st Sarah Alden; m. 2nd Desire (Doty) (Holmes) Sherman. He had, by his first wife,

  1. MYLES, d. Sept. 15, 1739; m. Experience Holmes.
  2. LORAH, m. Abraham Sampson.
  3. LYDIA, m. Isaac Sampson.
  4. MERCY, m. Caleb Sampson.
  5. ELIZABETH, m. Samuel Delano.
  6. SARAH, m. Benjamin Soule.
  7. EBENEZER, d. 1734; m. Hannah Sturtevant.

He had, by his second wife,

  8. DESIRE, b. May 5, 1689; m. Nathan Weston.
  9. THOMAS, b. Jan. 29, 1690; m. Mary Carver.
  10. ICHABOD, b. June 10, 1693; m. Phebe Ring.
  11. DAVID; no issue.

II — Josiah, d. March 19, 1690; m. 1st, Dec. 19, 1654, Mary Dingley, d. July 1, 1655; m. 2nd Sarah Allen. He had,

  12. JOSIAH, m. Sarah ——.
  13. MILES, m. Mehitabel (Cary) Adams.
  14. SAMUEL,
      m. 1st, Deborah Gates,
      m. 2nd, Mrs. Hannah Parke.
  15. ISRAEL, m. Elizabeth Richards.
  16. MARY, m. James Cary.
  17. LOIS, m. Hugh Calkins.
  18. MEHITABEL.
  19. MERCY.

* * * * * * *

RICHARD WARREN:
I — Mary, d. after Feb. 13, 1678; m. about 1628 or 29 Robert Bartlett, d. between Sept. 19 and Oct. 29, 1676, and had,
1. BENJAMIN, b. c. 1633.
   m. 1st, Susanna Jenny,
   m. 2nd, Sarah Brewster.
   m. 3rd, Cecilia ——.
2. REBECCA, m. 1649 William Harlow.
3. MARY,
   m. 1st, 1651, Richard Foster,
   m. 2nd, 1659, Jonathan Morey.
4. SARAH, m. Dec. 23, 1656, Samuel Rider.
5. JOSEPH, b. about 1639;
   m. Hannah Pope.
6. ELIZABETH, m. Dec. 26, 1661 Anthony Sprague.
7. MERCY, b. 1649-50; m. 1668 John Ivey.
8. LYDIA, b. June 18, 1648;
   m. 1st, John Barnaby,
   m. 2nd, John Nelson.

II — Ann, m. April 19, 1633, Thomas Little, d. March 1671-2, and had,
9. RUTH.
10. HANNAH, m. Stephen Tilden.
11. PATIENCE, b. 1639;
    m. Joseph Jones.
12. ISAAC, b. 1646;
    m. Bethiah Thomas.
13. MERCY, m. John Sawyer.
14. EPHRAIM, b. May 17, 1650;
    m. Mary Sturtevant.
15. THOMAS, unmarried.
16. SAMUEL, b. about 1657;
    m. Sarah Gray.

III — Sarah, m. John Cooke. (Issue; see Cooke family).

IV — Elizabeth, d. March 4, 1670; m. about 1635-6, Richard Church, b. about 1608, d. Dec. 27, 1668, and had,
17. ELIZABETH, m. Caleb Hobart
18. JOSEPH, b. 1637-8;
    m. Mary Tucker.
19. BENJAMIN, b. 1639-40;
    m. Alice Southworth.

20. NATHANIEL, m. Sarah Barstow.
21. CALEB,
    m. 1st, Joanna Sprague,
    m. 2nd, Deborah ——,
    m. 3rd, Rebecca Scotto.
22. CHARLES, d. Oct. 30, 1659;
23. PRISCILLA, b. 1645;
    prob. m. 1st, Samuel Talbot,
    prob. m. 2nd, John Irish.
24. ABIGAIL, b. June 22, 1657
    m. Samuel Thaxter.
25. RICHARD, d. y.
26. HANNAH, bapt. Aug. 8, 1657.
27. SARAH, m. James Burrows.
28. LYDIA, went to France.
29. DEBORAH, b. Jan. 27, 1656-7; d. Jan. 17, 1690.
30. MARY, d. April 30, 1662.

V — Abigail, m. Nov. 8, 1639, Anthony Snow, d. between Aug. 8 and Nov. 12, 1692, and had,
31. JOSIAH, m. Rebecca Barker.
32. LYDIA, m. Stephen Skiff (?)
33. SARAH, b. June, 1651;
    m. Joseph Waterman.
34. ABIGAIL, m. Michael Ford.
35. ALICE, b. Jan. 18, 1657;
    m. Robert Barker.
36. A son, b. March 25, 1665.

Vl — Nathaniel, b. 1624; d. betw. July 16 and Oct. 21, 1667; m. Nov. 19, 1645, Sarah Walker d. Nov. 24, 1700, and had,
37. RICHARD, b. 1646;
    m. Sarah ——.
38. JABEZ, b. 1647; d. unm.
39. SARAH, b. Aug. 29, 1649;
    m. John Blackwell.
40. HOPE, b. March 7, 1651-2;
    prob. d. unm.
41. JANE, b. Jan. 10, 1652-3;
    m. Benjamin Lombard.
42. ELIZABETH, b. Sept. 15, 1654; m. William Green.
43. ALICE, b. Aug. 2, 1656;
    m. Thomas Gibbs.
44. MERCY, b. Feb. 20, 1657-8;
    m. Jonathan Delano.

45. NATHANIEL, b. March 10, 1661-2; m. Phebe Murdock.
46. MARY, b. March 9, 1660-1; d. y.
47. JOHN, b. Oct. 23, 1663; d. y.
48. JAMES, b. Nov. 7, 1665; m. Sarah Doty.

VII — Joseph, b. 1626; d. May 4, 1689; m. c. 1651-2, Priscilla Faunce b. c. 1634, d. May 15, 1707, and had,
49. MERCY, b. Sept, 23, 1653; m. John Bradford.
50. ABIGAIL, b. 1655; d. y.
51. JOSEPH, b. Jan. 8, 1657; m. Mehitabel Wilder.
52. PATIENCE, b. March 15, 1660; m. Samuel Lucas.
53. ELIZABETH, b. Aug. 15, 1662; m. Josiah Finney.
54. BENJAMIN, b. Jan. 8, 1670; m. 1st, Hannah Morton, m. 2nd, Esther (Barnes) Cushman.

* * * * * * *

WILLIAM WHITE:

I — Resolved, d. about 1680; m. 1st Nov. 5, 1640, Judith Vassal, d. 1670; m. 2nd Oct. 5, 1674, Mrs. Abigail Lord. He had,
1. WILLIAM, b. April 18, 1642.
2. JOHN, b. March 11, 1644.
3. SAMUEL, b. March 13, 1646; m. Rebecca ——.
4. RESOLVED, b. Nov. 12, 1647; d. 1670.
5. ANNA, b. June 5, 1649; m. John Hayward.
6. ELIZABETH, b. June 4, 1652; m. prob. Obadiah Wheeler.
7. JOSIAH, b. Sept. 29, 1654; m. Remember Reed.
8. SUSANNAH, b. 1656; m. Uriah Johnson.

II — Peregrine, d. July 20, 1704; m. about 1647, Sarah Bassett, d. July 20, 1711, and had,
9. DANIEL, b. 1649; m. Hannah Hunt.
10. SARAH, m. Thomas Young.
11. MERCY, m. William Sherman.

12. JONATHAN, b. June 4, 1658;
    m. Esther Nickerson.
13. PEREGRINE, b. 1660;
    m. 1st, Susannah ——,
    m. 2nd, Mary ——.
14. SYLVANUS, m. Deborah ——.
    (No issue).

* * * * * * *

EDWARD WINSLOW:

I — Josiah, d. Dec. 18, 1680; m. 1657 Penelope Pelham, d. Dec. 7, 1703, and had,
  1. A daughter, b. 1658; d. y.
  2. ELIZABETH, b. April 8, 1654;
     m. Stephen Burton.
  3. EDWARD, b. May 14, 1667;
     d. y.
  4. ISAAC, b. 1670;
     m. Sarah Wensley.

II — Elizabeth, d. after 1694; m. 1st, Robert Brooks; m. 2nd, Sept. 22, 1669, George Curwen, b. Dec. 10, 1610, d. Jan. 3, 1684-5. She had,
  5. JOHN, d. Dec. 25, 1687.
  6. PENELOPE, b. Aug. 2, 1670;
     m. Josiah Walcott.
  7. SUSANNA, b. Dec. 10, 1672;
     m. 1st, Edward Lynde,
     m. 2nd, —— Wadsworth.
  8. GEORGE, b. 1674; d. before 1684.

(The End.)

A NATIONAL REGISTRY OF HUMAN PEDIGREES

From Articles of Incorporation of the Bureau of Military and Civic Achievement as provided in the Code of Laws enacted by Congress and approved by the President of the United States:

The term of its existence shall be in perpetuity.

The particular business and object of the organization will be

(a) To discover, collect, and perpetuate genealogical and historical data that relate to American families, and to provide a National registry of their pedigrees and coat armor in conjunction with the military and civic achievements of such registrant families.

(b) To render such data more readily available and the better to assure its preservation in perpetuity, to publish the same in chart and narrative forms for private archives and for filing in State and National Libraries; and to publish or promote such other works or publications as may be deemed advisable in furtherance of the objects and purposes herein set forth.

(c) To promote genealogical research and compilation of their pedigrees and vital statistics among American families for their historical and eugenic value.

(d) To inculcate that spirit of pride and devotion which every one owes to his family.

* * * * *

NOTE:

1 — A limited number of the pedigrees registered in the Historical Rolls of the Bureau of Military and Civic Achievement in its archives at Washington will, on arrangement of terms, be admitted to publication in a genealogical work to be issued in periodic volumes to the public archives of the states of the Union for filing permanently in

their State Archives, History Commissions, etc., and in the Library of Congress among its permanent collections. This multiplicity of depositories of safe keeping will assure preservation of the volumes in perpetuity, and make them locally available in every State so that they may be read a thousand or more years from now, similarly as we look back for names of our ancestors on the Rolls of Battle Abbey, or in the Domesday Book.

The work of the Bureau has a most important bearing upon the dignity and well-being of the nation. So much so that many people have said it ought to have been started a hundred or two years earlier.

2 — A Certificate of Achievement in the form of an Ancestral Chart is granted to families whose data are approved for publication. Their certification and approval for publication is also an evidence of the genuineness of the pedigree and distinctions claimed.

Families entitled to Coat Armor may by arrangement have their Arms blazoned (described) in the Yearbook, and portrayed on a Chart Pedigree.

Registration blanks sent on receipt of two cents to cover postage.

BUREAU OF MILITARY AND CIVIC ACHIEVEMENT
Washington, D. C.

PICKING UP THE MISSING LINKS

Running Out and Connecting Up Your Lines.

There seems to be an innate desire in mankind to know whence we come, and to collect and preserve data relating to our ancestry. Some may affect to regard this question with indifference, but those with a good pedigree have a natural pride of it.

The only way we can leave a history of ourselves, is to leave to posterity data telling of our origin — who we are, and what we did. Information that we do not have ourselves can only be had by searching it out.

To meet that contingency efficiently this Bureau maintains a corps of experienced genealogists, and through its Department of Extension picks up missing links, connects up and runs out lines to predetermined periods, or traces them to the remotest ancestor in this and foreign countries.

Coats of Arms are also searched for, and emblazoned.

Charges for research and heraldic work; preparation of chart pedigrees; publication of narrative pedigrees, and preparation of application papers for hereditary society membership, will be mailed on receipt of description of data to be furnished as a basis for the work desired.

Bureau of Military and Civic Achievement
Washington, D. C.

Lightning Source UK Ltd.
Milton Keynes UK
UKHW02f2005200318
319778UK00024B/443/P